Original title:
Stalk and Awe

Copyright © 2025 Creative Arts Management OÜ
All rights reserved.

Author: Lila Davenport
ISBN HARDBACK: 978-1-80566-606-6
ISBN PAPERBACK: 978-1-80566-891-6

Oft-Hidden Wonders

In shadows lurk a giggling gnome,
With a pointy hat and big red foam.
He trips on roots, then starts to dance,
While squirrels gather, they join the prance.

A lizard dons a tiny tie,
Sipping tea while passing by.
He winks at flowers, makes them blush,
As butterflies create a rush.

A hedgehog juggles acorns rare,
While badgers watch with vacant stare.
They bet on who will drop the prize,
The laughter echoes, fills the skies.

In this strange world, where quirks abound,
Each hidden gem can turn around.
So if you peek with a quirky grin,
You'll find the joy that lies within.

Enchantment in the Underbrush

In shadows deep where critters play,
A squirrel steals snacks, in a sneaky way.
The bushes giggle, leaves a-shake,
As frogs on lily pads make a splashquake.

A chatty bird sings tunes so sly,
While rabbits hop as if to fly.
Nature's stage is set for jest,
With laughter hidden, it's truly blessed.

Dance of the Unseen

In moonlit nights, the shadows twirl,
As fireflies wink in a dizzy whirl.
A raccoon dips low, then hops with glee,
While crickets chirp their own symphony.

With twigs as stage, the shrews keep score,
As beetles boogie on the forest floor.
Nature's ballet, so quirky and fun,
Each step a giggle, each leap a pun!

Echoes of the Overlooked

Behind the fence, a mouse meets a cat,
They share a joke, imagine that!
With noses twitching, they laugh in glee,
A daring duo, so wild and free.

The grasshoppers hop, a lively crew,
Debating which leaf has the best view.
They share their secrets, this breezy talk,
While ants march forth in a one-line walk.

The Lurker's Lament

Peeking around, a shadow grins,
As the mischievous raccoon spins.
With a scout's gaze, and whiskers wide,
He plots his caper, a sneaky glide.

A teddy bear waits in the softest nook,
With marshmallow dreams that draw a look.
He sighs as friends play hide and seek,
Nervous giggles turn bold and cheek.

Divine Overhearing

In the shadows, whispers flow,
Secrets tangled, spirits glow.
Eavesdropping on cosmic schemes,
Life's a joke, or so it seems.

A squirrel comments on the breeze,
While grass blades dance with glee.
Laughter bubbles from the trees,
Nature's jest, a subtle tease.

Moments Caught in Time

A cat stares down a passing car,
Its jeweled eyes, a strange avatar.
Time pauses, hearts skip a beat,
As if the world forgot its feet.

An awkward dance by a clownish bird,
Spinning tales with no spoken word.
The universe peeks and chuckles low,
At the oddities that come and go.

Capturing the Essence

A passing cloud puffs out a grin,
While raindrops giggle, ready to spin.
A moment caught, the charm awakes,
In every laugh, the skyline shakes.

A puppy chews on its own tail,
As birds tell tales with flapping sail.
Life's a sketch with vibrant strokes,
Painted bright with silly jokes.

The Poetry of Hidden Angles

Behind the bush, a giggle hides,
A late-night snack, the raccoon glides.
He steals a treat and strikes a pose,
In a dramatic, cheeky close.

A secret laugh beneath the moon,
Makes the garden twist and swoon.
In every corner, joy can find,
The humor weaves through tangled mind.

Mysterious Flutter

Beneath the moon, a shadow glides,
With fluttering wings, it softly hides.
A dance so clumsy, yet full of grace,
I chuckle as it flits from place to place.

The leaves rustle, a whisper's delight,
Strange critters laugh, what a silly sight!
A creature lands, then takes off once more,
Its antics leave me gasping, 'What's in store?'

Quiet Elegance of the Forest

In the stillness, a squirrel does prance,
With nut in hand, it twirls in a dance.
So poised and proper, it seems so refined,
Yet drops its treasure, oh how unkind!

A deer tiptoes past, with a haughty air,
It stops for a snack, but does it care?
With a flick of the tail, it's off like a flash,
Leaving behind only memories of a dash.

Bated Breath and Hidden Dreams

With bated breath, I spy through a crack,
A family of rabbits preparing a snack.
They nibble and chatter, what secrets they share,
Their munching sounds echo, filling the air.

From behind the bush, I let out a sneeze,
They scatter away, oh! What a tease!
But I'll sit and wait, with hope in my heart,
For more bunny drama is sure to start!

Trails of the Imagination

I wander the paths where the wild things play,
With thoughts so silly, I laugh all day.
What if a rabbit wore tiny shoes?
Or a bear that sings the blues?

Each step brings forth creatures, wondrous and bright,
Imagination's playground, what a delight!
I skip through the woods with a giggle and grin,
In this whimsical world, where the fun never ends.

Fantasia of the Unfamiliar

In the garden, gnomes dance and sway,
While pigeons put on a cabaret play.
A cat in a hat strums a tune,
Underneath the glowing moon.

A squirrel wearing shades rides a bike,
Hitching a ride on a playful hike.
While flowers giggle as bees sing loud,
The whole scene is just crazily proud.

Mice in tuxedos make quite a show,
As they serve cheese on a fancy plateau.
With laughter echoing through the trees,
It's a carnival of quirks, if you please!

The shrubs wear scarves, one polka dot,
While leaves debate which dance is hot.
Such nonsense can only exist,
In a dream we never planned—who could resist?

Glow of the Forgotten

An old toaster sings with rusty tunes,
While the clock does a jig under the moons.
A chair plays poker with old dusty books,
In this gathering of whimsical crooks.

A mop with a mustache winks with flair,
As the blender spins tales that fill the air.
The fridge tells jokes that chill to the bone,
While lost socks still seek their mate—a drone.

Glitter spills forth from a high, cracked vase,
As dust bunnies twirl in a comic grace.
The memories laugh, they don't seem to fret,
In the glow of what's lost, there's no regret.

Old toys in boxes recall a great game,
While marbles collide, we hear each name.
In a scrapbook of laughter, this time unbends,
And what we forget becomes our best friends.

The Riddle of the Undergrowth

In the thicket, a frog reads a map,
To find his way back from a nap.
A hedgehog with glasses jots notes,
While beetles hum in tiny boats.

Beneath a fern, a dance-off's begun,
Where worms boogie and laugh just for fun.
The grasshoppers wish they could really fly,
But they really just bounce, oh my oh my!

A snail draws sketches on a wet stone,
Imagining worlds he can call his own.
While a curious fox peeks from the bush,
And the fairies sprinkle glitter in a hush.

The ants hold meetings on who found the crumbs,
While crickets sing out like little drums.
In this undergrowth of riddle and jest,
Life's giggles emerge, and we are all blessed.

Mirage of Movement

A dancing dust cloud prances by,
While shadows join in without a shy.
A hammock sways to an unseen beat,
Factory of laughter, full of heat.

Trees in tuxedos twirl with the breeze,
As birds in bowties compose melodies.
An old bicycle glides like a ghost,
In this mirage, we marvel the most.

Someone once said that chairs can't dance,
But these ones sway, inviting a chance.
While flowers clap as the sun steps down,
In this cheerful chaos, let laughter abound.

Around us, the world teases with glee,
Where echoes of joy make us feel free.
In every step, a silly jest,
In this dance of life, we are truly blessed.

The Art of Silent Observation

In bushes thick, I take my stand,
Sipping tea, oh isn't it grand?
With twigs as friends, I spy about,
What's that noise? Is it a mouse, no doubt!

With careful steps, I creep along,
A cat-cum-detective, where I belong.
A squirrel points, a bird does sing,
"Hey! No peeking!" Oh, what a fling!

A shuffle here, a rustle there,
Collecting tales, I'm a truth or dare.
Who knew that grass could hold such glee?
Just look at them—silly, wild, and free!

In the end, it's all in the jest,
Being unseen is quite the quest.
With laughter bubbling, I'll return home,
As a sly observer, never alone!

In Pursuit of Shadows

Chasing shadows on the wall,
I tiptoe quietly, not to fall.
With each shift, my heart takes flight,
"Is that a shadow? Or just the night?"

I crouch behind a potted plant,
Pretending to be the world's best ant.
With careful moves, I plot, I plan,
To catch the light, not catch a tan!

In the kitchen, oh what a sight,
The toaster gleams, no need for fright.
A fork and spoon dance along the way,
"It's just me, shadows! Come out to play!"

I tumble, I roll, now I'm in the fray,
What's hiding behind that hay?
A giggle erupts, it's time to pause,
Shadows may flee, but my love for them, draws!

The Thrill of the Unnoticed

In the hallway, I make my round,
With unseen giggles in the sound.
A paperclip, what a funky find,
Perhaps it's my new friend, oh so blind!

Behind the curtains, in a twist,
I join a secret, made of mist.
Laughing softly at what I see,
Even my shadow winks at me!

Coffee's brewing, oh what a whiff,
I'm an invisible, hop-skip, and gift.
With every sip, a daring cheer,
Who could guess I'm lurking here?

At dusk I tiptoe back to my spot,
Unnoticed fun, it's all I got.
With a home full of whispers, my heart starts to race,
For cracking secrets, I've found my place!

The Dance of the Unseen

Underneath the disco lights,
I sway, unseen, with critters in tights.
A skunk in sequins, a raccoon in a cap,
We're all just groovin', what a cool trap!

The walls are alive with rhythm and jest,
Each footstep echoes, a wild fest.
While humans fumble in their dance of fate,
We twirl and whirl, isn't it great?

A sneaky fox, a hopping hare,
Twirling beats in the cool night air.
Sass and giggles fill the space,
Our secret raves, an unseen place!

With laughter and moonlight, we set the scene,
The dance floor sparkles, all so keen.
So here's to the unseen, the joy of the chase,
In the waltz of the night, we've found our place!

Veiled Intentions

In shadows they shiver, such mischief in mind,
Socks on their hands, oh, what will they find?
Sneaky as squirrels, they plot from afar,
Even the lamp seems to giggle and spar.

A wig on a broom and a hat from the cat,
Why, no one would question, it's silly and fat!
Rummaging through drawers that creak and that squeak,
Oh, what are they after? It's just hide-and-seek!

With giggles they tiptoe, in haste they will flee,
A fruitcake, a rubber duck, what could it be?
Each face in the mirror reflects their grand pranks,
As they scramble for treasure amidst all the flanks.

So next time you ponder a strange little sound,
Remember the misfits that dance all around.
In spaces where echoes of laughter collide,
The humor of secrets is marveled and tied.

In the Presence of the Unknown

A shadow slips past, what could it be now?
A cat wearing glasses? Oh, give it a bow!
Chimneys are laughing, the night's full of cheer,
Dancing on rooftops, or so it appears.

The toaster is buzzing, the fridge hums a tune,
What magic's afoot under the light of the moon?
Perhaps that old couch has a tale to regale,
Of couches who dream while the humans all bail.

With whispers and chuckles, the floorboards conspire,
What secrets they hold in the flickering fire!
A sock on the ceiling, a shoe on the floor,
In this house of wonders, who could ask for more?

When laughter erupts from the depths of your dreams,
You'll know you've been caught in the land of extremes.
So wander with glee through the shadows that tease,
In the festival of quirks, you'll find joy and ease.

Pursued by the Unseen

An echoing giggle, a rustle of leaves,
A rubber chicken rolls, and oh how it cleaves!
With friends in the bushes, they're ready to play,
Whispers and chuckles, they'll brighten your day.

A rubber glove flutters, it joins in the fun,
Pepper shakers dance, oh, don't they all run?
The cat gives a sigh, as it watches the chase,
This hunt for the silly takes you to a place.

Under the table, a foot reaches out,
A ticklish encounter brings forth a loud shout!
Scooping up cupcakes, a wild game to quell,
What wild, wearing laughter can hide oh so well?

So when you're alone, in the dimming of light,
Listen for giggles that joyfully spite.
For in every corner, in quiet retreat,
Lurks fun, like a jester, so nimble and fleet.

The Secrets We Keep

In corners so cozy, conspiracies brew,
A stash of old candies—the sweet and the skew!
Post-it notes giggle, they flap in delight,
What secrets are stirring in the dead of night?

As mugs gather dust, tales tumble and spin,
Of socks that went missing and where they have been.
Beneath the old staircase, a mystery waits,
Juggling the laughter while opening gates.

With blankets like capes, they take flight on a whim,
The couch is a castle, its purpose is grim.
Quests for lost trinkets, a battle of wits,
The laughter of bandits where silliness flits.

So come join the dance of the secrets we hold,
For in every chuckle, a memory's gold.
In corners and shadows, where giggles have leaped,
The stories of friends are forever well-kept.

Pathways to the Hidden

In the garden, something stirs,
A raccoon trip with clumsy purrs.
Sneaking snacks from my picnic plate,
Its cheeky grin seals its fate.

Behind the bushes, whispers grow,
A squirrel's dance puts on a show.
He leaps and bounces, what a sight,
Turning lunch into pure delight.

Underneath the porch, shoes mismatch,
I find a mouse and a hidden stash.
It twitches nose and darts away,
Leaving me with crumbs of dismay.

In the world beneath my feet,
I find the bugs have come to eat.
Their tiny feasts are quite the thrill,
Yet they find my snack far more than nil.

The Mystery Beneath the Stars

At night the stars begin to glow,
But what's that noise? It's rather low.
An owl hoots with a wink and flare,
As if to say, 'You've got no scare!'

A raccoon moonwalks by the shed,
With shiny eyes and clever head.
He's stealing snacks from the backyard bin,
With such finesse, he wears a grin.

The fireflies dance, they twinkle bright,
Bumping into friends in their flight.
They form a train—quite the odd crowd,
It's a glowing party, oh so loud!

Lying back, I see the show,
Under the stars where giggles flow.
Nature's humor, wild and free,
Keeps me laughing with glee.

Unveiling of Nature's Secrets

In the woods where shadows play,
A fox prances in a silly way.
With a flick of tail, it starts to strut,
I chuckle softly, that furry nut!

The rabbits hop in a funny line,
Chasing tails, oh so divine.
Each bound a leap of pure delight,
As they race through fading light.

Leaves rustle with a giggling sound,
A chorus of critters all around.
They dare to peek from their leafy bed,
With silly hats upon their head!

The whispers of the trees then say,
'Keep your eyes open, come what may.'
The antics of nature, a curious feat,
Bringing smiles to hearts, oh so sweet!

Secrets of the Wild

What's that lurking in the brush?
A little deer, oh what a rush!
It prances by, a graceful dance,
With goofy steps, it's quite a chance.

A beaver's building with sticks galore,
While ducks quack loud, they all implore.
"Join our game!" they seem to shout,
As they splash around without a doubt.

The woodpecker's knock, it's quite absurd,
As he tries to mimic a funny word.
Peck, peck, peck, it's a comedy show,
While squirrels chuckle, just watching the flow.

Nature's secrets, a laugh in disguise,
With each creature, a new surprise.
In this wild world, I cannot fall,
For the funny moments encompass all!

Where Curiosity Roams

In shadows, whispers dance and play,
With secrets hidden, come what may.
The dog peeks out, an eager spy,
A squirrel darts, oh my, oh my!

What's behind the garden fence?
A rogue raccoon? A cat, perhaps?
With every rustle, giggles bloom,
Each peek, a promise of cartoon doom!

Sneaky steps on creaky wood,
The flower pot gives me a good hood.
Is that a bird or just my hat?
I swear, I heard it—where's my cat?

The thrill of guessing fills the air,
What's in the bushes? A prankster bear?
Adventure calls with a playful grin,
Let's flip the plan, let's dive right in!

The Allure of Stealth

Sneaky sneakers on the ground,
I tiptoe past, without a sound.
Behind the curtain, eyes so wide,
I'm on a mission, nowhere to hide!

The cookie jar is my only goal,
But even shadows take a toll.
Glancing left, then peeking right,
Oh no! The dog is in my sight!

With stealthy moves, I grab a treat,
Munching silently, a tasty feat.
But crumbs betray my crafty ways,
As guilty glances earn dismayed gaze!

The chase is on, I drop and roll,
Life's a game, let's take control!
With giggles shared, the fun begins,
For every mischief, laughter wins!

Hushed Expectations

In a room where echoes dare,
I spot a sock that's lost somewhere.
My friend creeps in with sneaky eyes,
What mischief planned, oh what surprise!

The clock ticks slowly, hearts in tune,
A pop-out surprise? A party boon!
But instead a cat leaps with flair,
My snack is gone, oh how unfair!

With bated breath, we spy the door,
Anticipating a silly chore.
But when it swings, to our delight,
A birthday cake—what a sight!

Our laughter bursts, it's pure delight,
Expectations soar to dizzy height.
In each surprise, we find pure bliss,
Life's little twists, we wouldn't miss!

Beneath the Surface

Under the bridge, the waters flow,
A fishy tale begins to grow.
With rod in hand, we make our stand,
But the fish are clever—oh, ain't it grand?

They flip and flop, with sly intent,
In this watery stage, they're heaven-sent.
A tangle of lines and laughter shared,
Every splash leaves us unprepared!

The sun shines bright, we're all ablaze,
With searching eyes, in a fishy gaze.
But when we hook one, cheers erupt,
A jump, a twist—what luck, what luck!

The chase is on, we hold our breath,
With jokes exchanged, we toy with death.
Beneath the surface, life's a game,
In every catch, we find our fame!

Where Mystery Lingers

In shadows bright, a rabbit prances,
With socks on paws, oh what are the chances?
It twirls and leaps, a sight to see,
A dance that leaves us chuckling with glee.

Beneath the moon, a cat surveys,
With grand ideas and fanciful ways.
It plans a heist for some cheese and bread,
As squirrels conspire, filling its head.

Among the trees, a secret grows,
A snail in a hat, how bizarre, who knows?
It slides with style, a shell so chic,
While ladybugs giggle, and grasshoppers squeak.

Yet when dawn breaks, the fun does fade,
With sleepy yawns in the sunlit glade.
But tales of the night, with laughter and cheer,
Will keep us smiling, till next time, dear.

Beneath the Bramble

In tangled woods, where critters play,
A hedgehog spins, in a blustery ballet.
With tiny shoes and mischief in mind,
It pricks up the leaves, oh what a find!

A wise old owl in spectacles, too,
Misreads the map, oh what will it do?
It hikes through the thorns, head held so high,
In search of a snack, or perhaps a pie!

On tangling vines, a frog does strut,
In shiny boots, with a slight little gut.
It fancies a leap, but lands with a splash,
As the pond erupts in a whimsical crash.

With every twist, a giggle leads,
Nature's funny, with all its deeds.
We'll recount these tales, 'neath the bramble's glow,
A laugh or two, as the bright winds blow.

Enigmatic Presence

In the garden nook, with vibrant blooms,
A squirrel types on little things it assumes.
Wit in its paws, a laptop of nut,
It blogs about life and how to strut!

A curious cat, with a beret on its head,
Pretends to be famous, while seeking its bed.
It flicks its tail, full of charm and flair,
Yet dozes off, unaware of its air.

The polka-dot bug, a dazzling sight,
Hums to the rhythm of day turning night.
It plays the kazoo, as butterflies sway,
Oh, laughter abounds in this curious play.

In moments like these, where wonder thrives,
The foolish and funny, where each joy arrives.
With each silent pause, and a chuckle so bright,
Life's strange ballet dances into the night.

A Glimpse of the Unnoticed

A snail in a suit with a briefcase tight,
Heads to the office, what a curious sight!
It carries the weight of the world, you see,
On a path so slow, toward destiny.

The chubby raccoon, with its mask of delight,
Digs through the trash in the dark of the night.
It finds treasures rare, to flaunt and to show,
Like crowns made of foil, and string made to glow.

A dance of the fireflies, winking in sync,
Turn tables and twirl, as if on the brink.
With giggles of youth and laughter they beam,
Creating a spectacle like some wild dream.

So here's to the moments that slip through the day,
Where quirkiness lingers, and laughter will play.
In the odds and the ends, let's find joy comically,
Artfully unnoticed, in life's grand symmetry.

Steps Between the Trees

In the woods where mischief plays,
Tiny feet make sneaky ways.
Branches wave like eager hands,
Whispers tickle through the lands.

Frogs hop by, a daring cheer,
Squirrels pause, then disappear.
Come closer, bend down for a peek,
What creatures hide? Oh, the fun we seek!

A shadow flits, something spry,
Is it an elf, or just a fly?
With every step, giggles bloom,
Nature's stage, a lively room.

So tiptoe on, with gleeful grins,
In this dance, the laughter spins.
Among the trees, wild and free,
Adventure calls, just wait and see!

Intrigue Among the Leaves

Rustling whispers, a playful sound,
Secrets drift as we roam around.
Bright-eyed birds gossip in their flight,
While the squirrels plan a cheeky bite.

Leaves may shiver with a joke,
As acorns bounce, a tiny poke.
The wind giggles, can't hold it in,
Nature's jest? Oh, let's begin!

Shadow forms twist in fun ways,
Playing tricks like children's plays.
What's this riddle that nature weaves?
Let's unravel with fallen leaves!

Under the canopy, we laugh so loud,
In the heart of greens, we feel so proud.
Every nook hides a new delight,
Join the dance of the day and night!

The Art of Quiet Observation

In stillness, we spy a wiggly worm,
Pretending to be a tree's firm germ.
With careful eyes, we seek the sly,
Crafty critters that buzz and fly.

Mice in coats of muddy brown,
Waddle by wearing nature's crown.
With quiet chuckles, we blend and watch,
Moments of joy that nature can botch!

A butterfly flits in a dizzy dance,
We giggle softly, a secret glance.
Instead of hiding, come out to play,
Every creature has games to display!

So still we sit, beneath the trees,
Taking in life with the softest breeze.
In this playful, quiet scheme,
Nature's humor is the sweetest dream!

Veiled Curiosity

Behind each bush, what might we find?
An oddball critter? A rare kind?
A giggling gnome or fairy sprite,
To uncover what's hidden in twilight.

Peeking through branches, a baby deer,
Wide-eyed surprise, then it disappears.
Under leaves, a secret realm,
Imagine how it feels at the helm!

Shadows dance as dusk settles down,
Creepy creatures with mischievous frown.
With a hop and a skip, they join our game,
Laughter rings in this wild fame!

So pull back the petals, don't be shy,
Nature's magic will draw you nigh.
In playful pursuit of what's concealed,
Let curiosity be your shield!

Beneath the Canopy's Gaze

In a forest full of trees,
Where squirrels tease the breeze,
I tiptoe with a wobbly gait,
Afraid I'll find a bear on my plate.

Branches overhead tickle my eyes,
As I dodge a shower of wild pies,
A raccoon interrupts my flight,
He's planning a feast under moonlight.

The shadows join in silly dance,
As all the critters take a chance,
To leap and prance, to hop and swing,
Underneath the nighttime's bling.

With laughter echoing through the pines,
I join their antics, crossing lines,
For in this playful leafy maze,
It's hard to take things too serious these days.

Eyes in the Twilight

As dusk settles with a glowing grin,
The owls yodel, let the fun begin,
I'm peeking through tall grass and weeds,
Avoiding pranks like unwanted seeds.

A bunny hops, then stops to stare,
Funny how they don't seem to care,
I'm tiptoeing like I'm on a tightrope,
In hopes that I won't fall or elope.

The moon begins to chuckle bright,
As critters gather for a night flight,
Weaving tales of nights gone past,
While I wonder who'll be the last!

Underneath the stars so bold,
The laughter comes, some stories told,
In a world where shadows play,
I find myself hoping to stay.

Treading on the Edge of Mystery

With every step, a mystery brews,
Puddles of giggles, colors of blues,
I search for treasures and snacks to munch,
Dodging as I hear a sudden crunch.

A fox with sunglasses gives me a wink,
I'm bursting with laughter, can't help but think,
This forest is full of silly delight,
As squirrels juggle acorns out of sight.

Barefoot on the paths made of fluff,
Adventures here can never be tough,
Dancing with shadows, I spin around,
In this whimsical world, joy abounds.

Whispers of secrets float in the air,
While I try not to trip on a hare,
Each twist and turn, each cranny I find,
Leaves me chuckling, fresh in my mind.

The Quiet Pursuit

In the silence, mischief lurks,
Watchful eyes, are they friend or jerks?
Slinking behind a big old tree,
Oh, what trouble might there be?

A lizard lounges on a rock,
While I practice my stealthy walk,
But then I trip, a stumble loud,
Awakening the sleepy crowd.

Chirps and squeaks erupt in cheer,
As I scramble, wiping my fear,
I giggle at how I lost my grace,
In this enchanted, whimsical space.

With critter giggles echoing strong,
I'm reminded it's where I belong,
For each pursuit, though quiet it seems,
Is filled with laughter and silly schemes.

The Shroud of Enigma

In the shadows, things seem odd,
A squirrel dances, taking a nod.
A hat on a broom, what a prank,
Who left this here? Let's give it a crank.

The wind whispers jokes in my ear,
A flying fish, oh dear, oh dear!
A riddle wrapped in a cloak of delight,
Suspicions arise—was that couch a kite?

I saw a tree trying to bake,
It probably thought it was a cake!
I glanced closer, what did I see?
A raccoon hosting a wild jamboree!

Through the gloom, I felt the tease,
A singing mouse, "Please, oh please!"
It won't share secrets, we must beg,
But in this madness, we'll dance a leg.

Stillness of the Unseen

In the quiet, things look funny,
A snail on the run, isn't that sunny?
A ghost with a broomstick starts to sweep,
I'm giggling now, better not creep.

A shadow flickers, oh what a sight,
Is that a cat in a nap, or a knight?
With a cape made of cheese, it surely speaks,
I'll ask it for wisdom—in choppy peaks.

The sidewalk turned into a parade,
Rubber ducks quacking, what a charade!
I'm chuckling soft, taking a seat,
This quiet world can't be beat!

Some socks are dancing, twirling around,
Maybe they've finally found solid ground.
With my pants in a twist, I can't help but cheer,
For the stillness is busy, without a fear.

Intricate Layers of Life

A platypus wearing a chef's hat,
Created a sandwich from the family cat.
"I'm hungry," it quacked, "have some thyme,"
The joke's on us, it's lunchtime prime!

Eggplants gossip, it's quite the chatter,
They're growing wise—it really does matter.
With sunglasses on, they watch the sun,
Garden shenanigans, oh what fun!

A butterfly slips, it stumbles and laughs,
Landing on cabbage, but not in the class.
With outfits of color, they flutter about,
Creating a scene that's filled with clout.

Life's oddities don't just appear,
Underneath layers, they all draw near.
Let's celebrate mischief; that's our find,
For happiness echoes in chaos combined.

Curiosity's Lament

What's that wiggling in the grass?
A puppet show with a class of sass!
With ants in tuxedos, they take the stage,
As the world around them turns a page.

A cat on a violin tries to play,
Neighbors gather, "Is that a ballet?"
A toast to the laughter that fills the air,
While they spin in circles without a care.

A hedgehog whispers a secret to me,
"Every leaf's hiding a jubilee."
With a grin on its face, it scurries along,
In the weirdness of life, we all belong!

So let's dance with the odd, embrace the surprise,
For in every twist lies laughter's reprise.
Curiosity's here, and it's not going away,
Join the absurd and let's frolic all day!

Whispers in the Shadows

In the dark, they tiptoe near,
Socks of stripes, all full of cheer.
With giggles low, they peek and play,
Mischievous spirits on display.

Phantom feet with silly prance,
They trip and stumble, what a dance!
A whispered joke, a playful curse,
Just hope they don't make things much worse!

Underneath the moonlit gloom,
They scamper fast, they sneak and zoom.
A grand parade of polka dots,
Invisible but tying knots.

When dawn arrives, they leave their mark,
Laughing at their midnight spark.
Yet all that's left, a tiny trace,
Just giggles lingering in the space.

Secrets of the Silent Woods

In quiet woods where whispers dwell,
A sneaky squirrel weaves its spell.
With acorns stashed and eyes so wide,
It's quite a party, come and hide!

Behind the trees, a flicker glows,
A badger wearing mismatched clothes.
It shares a tale of far-off dreams,
With woodland friends and silly schemes.

The rabbits laugh, the owls blink slow,
As branches rustle from below.
What's that rustling in the brush?
Just playful paws, in a merry rush!

With every rustle, secrets blend,
A giggling crowd they can't offend.
Nature's jesters, quiet jest,
Leave footprints where the fun is best.

The Watcher's Serenade

Up in the trees, a gaze so sly,
A raccoon spots a passerby.
With twinkling eyes, it starts to sing,
Of midnight snacks and silly things.

"Hey there, friend, come take a peek,
The night is young, let's play hide and seek!"
A chorus calls from branches high,
Silly sounds that fill the sky.

A giggle here, a whistle there,
The forest knows, it's quite the flair.
With every note, they tumble down,
An oddball troupe wearing a crown!

At dawn they scatter, playtime ends,
But laughter lingers with the winds.
In secret spots, the fun remains,
And echoes of their antics reign.

Hidden Footprints

What's that rustle in the leaves?
Just tiny feet that dance and weave.
An army of ants in bright parade,
Marching on, they're not afraid!

Each little foot, a tiny trooper,
With comical strides, an army super!
Tickling grass and making cheer,
They giggle softly, come right here!

A fox peeks out, its tail a flare,
With fnniy wiggles, swinging in the air.
It joins the fun, a sleek ballet,
In this wild woodland cabaret!

But as the sun dips down to hide,
They pause their game, with smiles wide.
For in their trails, hee-hee, they choose,
To leave behind a world of shoes!

Secrets Wrapped in Leaves

In the forest, a rustle and snap,
A squirrel thinks it's quite a trap.
With acorns under tiny paws,
He giggles at all the hidden flaws.

Behind a bush, a rabbit peeks,
His twitching nose, the laugh it seeks.
In this green maze, secrets hide,
As nature's jesters laugh and glide.

High above, a bird does tease,
Dropping twigs, oh what a spree!
The forest floor is littered well,
With gossip that the branches tell.

Nature's playhouse, delight and cheer,
Where every sound brings laughter near.
Among the leaves, joy takes flight,
Under the sun, a silly sight.

Silent Pursuit

A fox in sneakers, oh what a sight,
Chasing shadows, dodging left and right.
With a hop and a skip, he plans his path,
While a startled deer lets out a laugh.

The owl, wise but still quite coy,
Watches the chase, an amused old boy.
With each twist, he shakes his head,
At the absurdity of the woodland thread.

From the bushes, a badger rolls,
Dreaming of sweets, ignoring the goals.
As the chaos unfolds with great delight,
The forest seems to giggle in the night.

Oh, the thrill of the invisible race,
As furry friends change the pace.
In the underbrush, the laughter swells,
In this silent chase, no one truly dwells.

Shadows in the Grove

In the grove, shadows play tag,
A sneaky raccoon grabs his bag.
With a wink and a crafty paw,
He bends the rules of nature's law.

A shadow flits on the forest floor,
While trees chuckle, calling for more.
An ant in a hurry, a snail at his pace,
Each one joins in this wild race!

As dusk falls, the giggles arise,
Among the branches, the laughter flies.
Twisted forms in the fading light,
Keep the spirits alive through the night.

So join the fun, let shadows glide,
In this funny grove, where joy won't hide.
With every leap, let your heart roam,
In shadows, you'll find a lively home.

Whispers Beneath the Canopy

Beneath the leaves, whispers abound,
A chipmunk shares secrets all around.
With every nibble, stories grow,
Of nutty mishaps, oh what a show!

A raccoon chimes in, with a wink,
"Did you see the frog? He can't even blink!"
Laughter bubbles among the trees,
As squirrels join in, dancing with ease.

The canopy sways, a laughter song,
Where even the shy ones feel they belong.
A playful breeze stirs up a cheer,
In this leafy world, smiles disappear.

So listen close, let nature's jest
Bring joy and laughter, that's the best.
With every whisper, life's a play,
In this green theater, come what may.

Beyond Vision's Reach

In the garden, I did peek,
But the gnome just made me freak.
He waved his arm, quite a show,
Was it magic? I don't know!

With binoculars aimed at a bee,
It buzzed away, just to tease me.
What a chubby little thing,
Thinking it's a real royal king!

Caught a squirrel in my sights,
Stealing nuts, oh what delights!
I giggled as he tried to hide,
With acorns snatched, he took a ride!

So if you think you are unseen,
Just look around; there's much to glean.
Life's a show, a comedic scheme,
In every corner, there's a dream!

The Sound of Watching

I heard a rustle, what could it be?
A mouse or maybe a tiny flea?
But it turned out to just be air,
My heart thumped loud; I felt despair!

I leaned in close to hear the laugh,
Turned out to be a photograph!
Of my cat, plotting with a grin,
Scheming ways to sneak back in.

The neighbor's dog barks like a beast,
But secretly, he's a feathered feast.
Chasing shadows, nothing you'll find,
While his owners just roll their minds!

In a world where stillness can mislead,
Every hush has a tale to heed.
So listen well, my curious friend,
In silence, the fun never ends!

The Nature of Intrigue

The cookie jar sits on the shelf,
I swear it's shaped just like an elf.
With every nibble, a new clue,
Is it magic or just a rue?

A cat climbs high, just out of reach,
Uncovering secrets, what a speech!
He ponders life while perched on high,
Does he think humans are a pie?

Then there's a shadow slipping past,
A little ninja, moving fast.
I swear it wore a tiny hat,
Furry friends joining for a chat!

In the end, it's all just play,
Life's a jester, come what may.
So gather round, let giggles spring,
For in each whisper, joy will cling!

Where Shadows Reside

Where shadows dance and giggle bright,
I spotted one in morning light.
A funny face, all out of whack,
With arms that flail and a big, loud crack!

Twirling 'round the chair with flair,
I caught my dog giving me a stare.
He knows the mischief I hold dear,
All those wild tricks that bring good cheer!

A tap on glass, a ghostly knock,
'Twas just my sister playing the clock.
With laughter echoing all around,
Shadows speak without a sound!

So join the fun, let shadows play,
In this dance, we laugh all day.
Spin the tales of jest and glee,
For life's a stage, just wait and see!

Traces of a Hidden Path

In the woods, a squirrel prances,
Hiding nuts in odd romances.
Behind the tree, a giggle grows,
Guess who's watching? No one knows!

Leaves crunch softly, footsteps near,
A funny whisper fills the cheer.
The path reveals a secret laugh,
Is it a prank or nature's gaffe?

Tiny footprints, much too small,
Maybe it's a daring call.
Who left these signs? What could it be?
To solve the riddle is key for me!

With a wink and a little dash,
The chase begins, a hurried flash.
Follow the giggles, hear the sound,
On this hidden path, fun is found!

Murmurs of the Uninvited

In a corner, whispers weave,
Who's that lurking? Can't believe!
Behind the curtain, a friend waits,
Bouncing joy, like paper plates!

Invisible chatters fill the air,
Why are they here? Do they dare?
Sneaky giggles break the night,
Unseen guests bring pure delight.

Under the table, hiding low,
Poking fun, putting on a show.
With prankish joy, they throw a bash,
Watch your snacks, they're lightning fast!

As the moonlight starts to glow,
Uninvited? No, they steal the show!
With laughter ringing, bright and bold,
Their cheeky tales must be retold!

Shadows that Dwell

In the night, shadows play games,
Who's that peeking? What are their names?
Under the streetlamp, they twirl and sway,
Dancing in rhythm, come out and play!

Characters shift, a comical fright,
Turning a cat into a knight!
Their giggling echo, a festive tease,
As they hide behind the swaying trees.

Peeking from corners, trying to blend,
Not so perfect, it's hard to pretend.
Watch as they leap, with bounces so bold,
These shadows share stories, funny and told!

In the dark, where secrets reside,
The shadows are friends, come take a ride.
With chuckles and giggles, they bow and bend,
In the quiet of night, they surely transcend!

Silhouettes in the Mist

Fog rolls in, secrets unfold,
Silhouettes dance, a sight to behold.
With clumsy grace, they trip and sway,
In this misty party, they lose their way!

Tall and short, they twist like vines,
In the shroud, they do their lines.
With arms like octopuses, they reach for stars,
Awkward moves, they're simply bizarre!

Laughter bubbles in the haze,
Creeping softly with funny displays.
Hats tipped low, voices a song,
In this cloudy riddle, they cannot go wrong!

So join the parade, don't be shy,
In your own silhouette, give it a try!
With giggles to share, fun to persist,
In the misty glow, you can't resist!

The Thrill of the Unknown

In the tickle of twilight's whisper,
I tiptoe where shadows fester.
What lurks behind the garden gate?
A raccoon? A cat? Or something great?

With a flashlight, I dare to peep,
a night of secrets that won't let me sleep.
The rustle's a mystery, a giggle-fest,
I flee from the bushes—I won't take that test!

I spy with my little eye something absurd,
a twig on the ground that could be a bird!
Each crack of a branch ignites my delight,
for every whisper could turn into fright!

In the thrill of the night, curiosity sings,
as I dart through the grass where mischief begins.
Laughter bubbles up with each tiny scare,
the unknown's a joke that dances in air.

Beyond the Eye

Peeking through the curtains of a sunny day,
I spot a wild squirrel, ready to play.
With acorns galore and a baffling plan,
he dances like no one knows he can!

In the breeze, the twigs do a delicate jig,
as my furry friends start their fun little gig.
They leap from the branches, mischief afoot,
while I sit here grinning, tying my boot.

And if I should whistle, they halt in surprise,
giving me looks with those bright, curious eyes.
The world of the critters, a stage of delight,
of clumsy performances that last through the night.

Nature's a circus with a show every day,
and all I can do is watch and convey.
With a chuckle, I witness their wild little spree,
a comedy act set in front of a tree.

Those Who Watch

Behind the tall grass, the watchers reside,
with wide-open eyes and no place to hide.
A parade of ants marches like soldiers,
while beetles debate the weight of their boulders.

I giggle at creatures imbued with such charm,
a snail on a quest causing no kind of harm.
And over there, on the tallest tall stone,
a frog croaks a tune like he's never alone!

Hark, what's that? A rat with a flare,
a dance on the pavement like it hasn't a care.
Impossible acrobatics, right under my nose,
I can't help but snicker at their silly repose.

They prance and they prattle with no sense of fear,
as I take notes, my laughter sincere.
For in this vast world so wondrously free,
it's the watchers that watch and laugh right with me.

Lullabies of the Leaves

In the canopy high, the leaves play a tune,
as they sway in the breeze, under the light of the moon.
Each rustle a melody, a symphonic delight,
a concert of whispers sauntering through night.

An owl gives a hoot, a comedic refrain,
bouncing off branches like drops of soft rain.
The flicker of fireflies becomes a soft show,
while crickets provide the percussion with flow.

I lay on the ground, with a grin on my face,
listening to nature's enchanting embrace.
Though no one can see the sweet banter I hear,
I giggle with joy, feeling utterly clear.

In the lull of the leaves, humor stirs deep,
as creatures of night sing the world into sleep.
I imagine their dance, and I chuckle away,
because every night's magic comes out to play.

Hushed Expectations

In the garden, whispers creep,
As bugs in tuxedos plan a sweep.
Laughter hides behind the leaves,
While ants perform their prancing eaves.

A squirrel wears a tiny crown,
Dancing with acorns, spinning 'round.
The petals giggle, colors bright,
As shadows plot their silly flight.

Eclipsed by the Wild

A hedgehog dons a cap of grass,
With tiny glasses, thinks he's grand,
The moonlight winks upon his face,
While critters join, a quirky band.

Raccoons with masks, they play at night,
Swiping snacks, a merry sight.
The owls hoot, a comical cheer,
As mischief brews, drawing near.

An Uncharted Path

A turtle maps his slow ascent,
With jellybeans to mark each bend.
The snail's his guide, but wears a frown,
As they discover wonders down.

The mushrooms dance and sing off-key,
In this wild place, they feel so free.
With every step, a funny twist,
A quest for giggles, none can resist.

Revelations in the Rustle

The leaves conspire with cheeky haste,
As squirrels play tag with nuts in waste.
The breeze brings gossip from afar,
Of mice in suits, a quirky star.

Through rustling tales, the whispers fly,
Of toes in puddles, and frogs nearby.
A world awash with silly themes,
Where laughter blooms, and nonsense gleams.

Observations from the Edge

In the shadows, I peek with glee,
A squirrel twirls, so sprightly and free.
It thinks it's a ninja, so sly and spry,
While plotting to steal my sandwich, oh my!

The trees all whisper, their secrets a tease,
As I trip on a root, say, 'Oh, not again, please!'
A frog in the pond croaks a tune so absurd,
It sounds like a cat that just swallowed a bird.

I watch as the ants march, a bustling parade,
Each one with a job, no time for charade.
They lift crumbs so big, like their muscles are flexed,
Meanwhile, I just sit, completely perplexed!

With giggles and gasps, I take in the view,
Nature's a circus; I'm laughing, it's true.
I'll mingle with critters, just him and just her,
For every odd moment's a joke, so astir!

Beneath the Veil of Green

Beneath the broad leaves, a sight to behold,
A snail slinks by, with a shell made of gold.
Its pace is a joke, oh, what a slow dance,
While I'm sipping soda, it's my quirky chance!

In the grass blades, a worm wobbles near,
A wrinkled old fellow, yet full of good cheer.
He wiggles and jiggles, a curious sight,
While the bugs all applaud, 'What a marvelous night!'

The daisies are gossiping, petals aglow,
'Have you seen the squirrel? He's quite a show!'
As the sun starts to dip, the headlines do grow,
'Local critters unite for the comedy show!'

Under canopies soft, nature's laughter blooms,
In this wild theater, we share all the rooms.
Each creature a player, in this green charade,
With joy and with giggles, we dance unafraid!

Silence that Speaks

In the quiet of dusk, the whispers unfold,
A rabbit's big ears wiggle, truly bold.
It hears every rumor, each rustle and snap,
As it munches on clovers, its favorite snack.

Silence descends, yet so much is said,
While owls cast their spells from their perch, overhead.
An awkward crow caws, like a cat with a sore,
As it flaps and it stumbles, demanding a floor.

The crickets start chirping a secretive tune,
While fireflies dance like the stars, oh so soon.
With giggles and snickers, they light up the night,
In the hues of the shadows, everything's bright.

So here in the calm, a party takes flight,
Beyond all the quiet, there's joy day and night.
With laughter enduring, in silence we glee,
In the whispers of nature, we find harmony!

The Unfolding Mystery

A puzzling conundrum unfolds by the stream,
What's that in the water? It sparkles and gleams.
Could it be treasure, or perhaps a good fish?
Nay, just a big boot—it's my biggest wish!

The duck floats by, nonchalant yet astute,
Wearing a scowl, in search of a fruit.
He quacks some dry jokes to the reeds that he spies,
While butterflies flutter, offering sighs.

In the bushes, a rustle, the lore starts to grow,
What creature is lurking? Oh, do tell me, though!
Is it a big monster, or just a lost shoe?
The thrill of the hunt leaves me giggling, it's true!

With each twist and turn, the plot thickens here,
Nature's absurdities bring joy, that's quite clear.
And in this grand tale, I'm the star of the show,
For every wild laugh is a mystery that flows!

The Dance of Perception

In the woods, the shadows wiggle,
A squirrel's jig makes me giggle.
It twirls and spins, full of flair,
I laugh as it leaps through the air.

A chipmunk joins with funky moves,
They dance, as if they've got something to prove.
I clap my hands and stomp my feet,
What a party, oh what a treat!

The leaves all rustle, join the beat,
Nature's rhythm is pretty neat.
With every twirl and silly prance,
I can't help but join the dance.

In this wild show of cheeky glee,
Who'd have thought I'd be a VIP?
With every wiggle, twist, and shout,
I dance along, without a doubt.

Curved Paths of Discovery

Down the path, a crooked line,
I wander, feeling simply fine.
A rabbit hops then skips away,
It winks at me, in bright display.

Around the bend, a lizard slides,
Wearing shades, it stylishly glides.
I chuckle loud, it's quite the sight,
This fashionista, oh so bright!

A squirrel quips and steals a nut,
It scurries off, what a cut!
With every twist, a new delight,
These forest antics feel just right.

Oh, the joy in nature's maze,
Each quirky friend deserves a praise.
Together we roam, quite the crew,
In this laughter, life feels new.

Vigil in the Underbrush

In the thicket, a lookout stands,
An owl stares with curious plans.
It hoots a tune, a cryptic song,
I ponder why it's there so long.

With bated breath, I keep my eyes,
On little bugs in silly disguise.
One does a flip, a brave ballet,
I can't help but laugh at their play.

A hedgehog rolls with quirky grace,
Trying hard to win this race.
Its spines are sharp, but heart is true,
Winning feels like nothing new.

Underbrush vigil, all around,
Nature wears a silly crown.
Every critter has its role,
To bring us joy, that is the goal.

Sights Beyond the Ordinary

I peek through branches with a grin,
A raccoon's party about to begin.
With tiny hats and treats in tow,
They welcome me to the wild show.

Each critter brings a silly snack,
Chirps and chatters, I fall back!
With popcorn flies and berry cakes,
These woodland friends, what fun they make.

Through leafy windows, giggles flow,
Tabbing into this nature show.
They're showcasing talents galore,
Stand-up acts? Who could ask for more!

In every corner, laughter spreads,
Beneath the trees, where joy embeds.
This secret realm, so fun and bright,
Turns ordinary into pure delight.

The Unseen Watcher

In the bushes, there's a face,
With a grin that's hard to place.
Peeking out from leafy green,
What a sight, it's quite the scene!

Blades of grass begin to shake,
Wonder if it's a prank to make.
A squirrel snickers from a tree,
Is it laughing just at me?

Underneath the picnic spread,
Sandwiches all slowly bled.
The unseen watcher works on snacks,
Filling up on crumbs and cracks!

With a chuckle and a point,
Laughter is the main joint.
Out in nature, what a crook,
Who knew bushes had a nook?

Echoes in the Wilderness

Whispers bounce where shadows play,
What's that noise? It's loud today!
Is that a deer or just my friend?
Every sound, it has its bend!

Branches snapping, laughter flows,
Echoes dance where nobody goes.
A bear might be but it's just Dave,
Trying hard to act so brave.

Rustling leaves, a racket grows,
"Stay quiet!" just a voice that knows.
But the giggles would betray,
The secrets of the woods today!

In the wild, too much fun,
Even owls can't seal the pun.
With each echo, jokes arise,
Nature's laughter, a pure surprise!

Gaze of the Hidden

Peering from behind the bark,
A raccoon plots before it's dark.
With its eyes aglow like beads,
Seeking out those tasty leads!

I swear I saw it wink at me,
Was that a laugh, or just some glee?
Hiding there, it takes a stance,
Oh, what luck, let's join the dance!

As it rolls into a pile,
That sneaky glance, oh what a style!
With a swagger, it's quite the charmer,
Grabbing all the snacks like a farmer!

Playful pranks and cheerful tricks,
Who knew nature had such kicks?
With a giggle and a squeal,
The hidden watcher's quite the deal!

Moonlit Footprints

Underneath the silver light,
Footprints dance, what a sight!
Are they human, or a hare?
Or perhaps a sneaky bear?

With each step, the giggles grow,
Moonlit paths where fun flows.
Through the grass, they prance and leap,
Quiet now, don't wake the sheep!

Marking trails with smiles bright,
Chasing shadows, oh what a fright!
Tripping over roots and rocks,
Nature's games outfox the clocks!

Laughter echoing through the night,
Who knew this could be such a delight?
Footprints lead to joy and cheer,
Moonlit memories year after year!

Nature's Hidden Narratives

Whispers from the shyest hare,
Tales of mischief on the air.
Squirrel steals a nut or two,
Laughing as it darts from view.

Pigeons plotting from above,
Throwing crumbs like they're in love.
Gossip flows among the trees,
Who's dating who, oh what a tease!

A chipmunk's secret stash revealed,
Peeking where the leaves are peeled.
Frogs croak jokes with utmost glee,
Nature's roguish comedy!

Underneath the moonlight bright,
Fireflies dance, a flashing sight.
With woodland critters in the fray,
Laughter echoes through the play.

Secrets in the Silence

Mice mess with the cat's big feet,
While owls laugh from their high seat.
A whisper curls through the grass,
As ants embark to make a pass.

When shadows flicker in the night,
A raccoon's antics give a fright!
Nature's whispers, secrets spill,
In the stillness, there's a thrill.

By the pond, frogs sing a tune,
Confessions made beneath the moon.
With chuckles shared among the reeds,
Their riotous laughter plants new seeds.

In the hush, there's mischief too,
As squirrels steal the birdseed hue.
A chorus of giggles in the park,
Sings of life's wild, whimsical arc.

Eyes in the Foliage

Peeking out from leafy beds,
Chirping secrets in their heads.
Bunnies giggle at the sight,
Of a cat that's lost its fright.

A pair of eyes from leafy greens,
Spy on all the silly scenes.
Squirrels plotting wild pranks,
Rattling leaves as they give thanks.

In the bushes, sounds arise,
Caterpillars dance under skies.
Nature's comedy on display,
With chuckles echoing all the way.

As daylight fades to twilight gold,
Mice retell every tale they've told.
In the trees, the whispers grow,
They share the laughter, stealing the show.

Footfalls in the Twilight

Pitter-patter on the ground,
Critters sneaking all around.
In the twilight's softer shade,
They join the game that's played.

A thump! A bump! A dash, a dive!
Rabbits hop and seem alive.
With every step, a giggle springs,
In the dusk where mischief sings.

Owls hoot loud in playful jest,
While fireflies join the quest.
Every footfall marks the fun,
As day gives way to the night-run.

Rustling leaves and sneaky moves,
Through the woods, the laughter grooves.
With every shadow, stories grow,
Children of the night in tow.

Nature's Hidden Marvels

In the garden, a worm does dance,
Wiggling freely, a funny chance.
A snail on a leaf, so slow and wise,
Looks like it's plotting to reach for the skies.

A puppy in grass, what a sight!
Chasing his tail with all of his might.
The daisies giggle, blades of green sway,
As the world spins round in a humorous way.

Bees in their suits are buzzing about,
Swapping secrets with flowers, no doubt.
The hedgehog snickers, rolled up snug tight,
Watching the antics of frogs in their plight.

In the chaos of nature, laughter is found,
From the smallest of critters to the trees all around.
We stumble and fumble, we laugh and we fall,
Nature's surprises bring joy to us all.

The Haunting Beauty of the Known

The shadows dip low, grinning wide,
A raccoon in a mask, swift as a slide.
With each scurrying paw, he joins the fun,
In the moon's soft glow, he's always on the run.

Owls hoot softly, they're whispering tales,
Of midnight adventures and ghostly trails.
A cat on a fence seems to know it all,
With a twitch of its tail, it sits proud and tall.

The wind tells secrets that make us chuckle,
As it tickles the leaves and bends every buckle.
A squirrel in mischief, with acorn in tow,
Races past shadows, just putting on a show.

The night is alive, with giggles and frights,
As critters emerge for their playful delights.
We bask in the thrill of the known and the whimsical,
In the echo of laughter, life seems so simple.

Rustle of the Unseen

In the underbrush, rustling brings cheer,
A dancing leaf, as if it could hear.
Whispers of creatures scurry and skitter,
Every crackle and pop adds a laugh to the litter.

A shadow flits by, quick as a wink,
Could it be magic, or just a pink drink?
The branches quiver, a slight little tease,
As wind giggles softly between trees.

Caterpillars wear tiny top hats,
Zooming around, dodging swooping bats.
With a wobble and wiggle, their party ignites,
Celebrating the nighttime with giggles and bites.

Mischief abounds in this hidden domain,
Nature's pranks light up like champagne.
With eyes full of wonder, we seek and believe,
In the rustle of unseen, there's joy to receive.

Chasing Shadows

A shadow on the wall starts to bend,
A kitty with stealth, oh what a trend!
She pounces and leaps, then slips on the floor,
Chasing her shadow, begging for more.

The sun plays tricks, making us grin,
With whimsical shapes that dance and spin.
A flicker of laughter as we trip in delight,
As shadows twist their way through the night.

Puppies run circles, barking with glee,
Their tails a-spinning, so wild and free.
Chasing the shadows that flicker and dart,
Each leap and each tumble, a comical art.

In the game of light, we join in the chase,
With giggles echoing, a jubilant race.
Every twist and turn, a new giggling sound,
In the chase of the shadows, joy can be found.

www.ingramcontent.com/pod-product-compliance
Lightning Source LLC
Chambersburg PA
CBHW051640160426
43209CB00004B/726